# The Secret Bay

Kimberly Ridley

Illustrated by Rebekah Raye

TILBURY HOUSE
PUBLISHERS

*creating worlds between covers*

great egret

marsh periwinkle

American oystercatcher

hermit crab

Atlantic horseshoe crab

smooth cordgrass

mummichog

2

You'll find me right here, where river meets ocean—
shining and muddy and always in motion.

Grass, mud, and water might be all that you see,
but don't be fooled—there is much more to me!

river otter

red knot

raccoon

black-crowned night heron

blue crab

American oyster

## What's an Estuary?

An estuary is a water body partly enclosed by land, where fresh water from one or more rivers mixes with salt water from the ocean, making *brackish* or mildly salty water. Most estuaries are the tidal mouths of rivers, and are saltier with seawater at high tide when the ocean fills them up, and less salty at low tide when there is more river water in the mix. The moon's gravitational pull on the ocean causes tides to rise and fall about twice each day in most estuaries, so they are places of constant change.

Some Native American tribes called estuaries "the Between-Lands" because they are part water and part land, including salt marsh and tidal flats. Many kinds of fish, other sea creatures, birds, mammals, and insects rely on estuaries as breeding, feeding, and resting places.

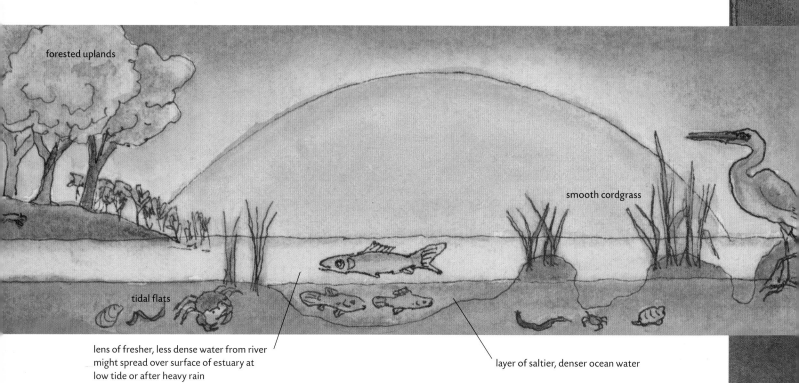

forested uplands

smooth cordgrass

tidal flats

lens of fresher, less dense water from river might spread over surface of estuary at low tide or after heavy rain

layer of saltier, denser ocean water

You can call me a bay, a sound or lagoon,
but one thing's for sure—I'm ruled by the moon.

I am an estuary, a place shaped by the tides,
and you won't believe all the secrets I hide.

5

I make much more food than even a farm,
and protect baby fishes from all kinds of harm.

I clean up the water, save houses from storms,
and host a parade of jazzy life forms.

## People and Estuaries

Estuaries are among the most productive ecosystems on earth. One acre of salt marsh along an estuary can produce up to ten tons of organic matter in a year—much more than an acre of farmland.

Up to 75 percent of the fish and shellfish we eat use estuaries as nurseries. Estuaries also provide *ecosystem services* that support all life. They filter pollution from rivers and ocean water, protect coastal land and communities from flooding and ocean storms, and provide habitat for fish, birds, and other wildlife.

Humans depend on estuaries for habitat and food, too, as well as for jobs and recreation. More than 60 percent of the world's people live on estuaries in cities such as Manhattan, San Francisco, and Tokyo, which was originally called "Edo" for estuary.

mummichog

With sunshine in springtime, salt water, and goop,
I stir up big batches of green plankton soup.

It feeds lots of sea life, which then can feed you—
every time you eat crab cakes or slurp seafood stew.

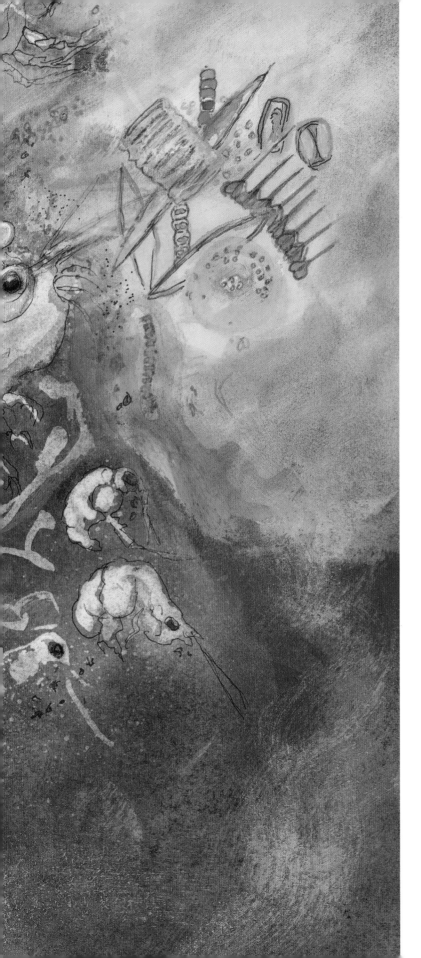

## Plankton Soup

One drop of estuary water can hold thousands of plankton—speck-sized animals and microscopic plants. *Zooplankton* are tiny floating animals that drift with the currents. Most are less than two millimeters or a tenth of an inch long, barely big enough to be seen with the naked eye. *Phytoplankton* are one-celled microscopic floating plants such as diatoms that look like green-gold jewels under a microscope. They are even smaller than zooplankton. They sometimes link together in chains but are still too small to be seen with the naked eye.

Phytoplankton make their own food from sunlight—just as plants on land do—and they multiply like crazy in spring, sometimes tinting the ocean and estuaries green. Without phytoplankton, there would be no fish in the sea, because these plants are the base of the ocean food web. Phytoplankton also produce about half of the oxygen we breathe. (The other half comes from plants on land.)

There are many kinds of zooplankton. Some, such as shrimp-like *copepods*, remain zooplankton throughout their lives Others are the newly hatched larvae of crabs, barnacles, lobsters, clams, mussels, sea stars, sea urchins, snails, and other animals that drift for a few weeks before settling to the bottom and *metamorphosing* (transforming) into miniature versions of the adult animals. Some zooplankton are *herbivores*, eating phytoplankton just as cows graze on grass, and some are *carnivores*, eating other zooplankton.

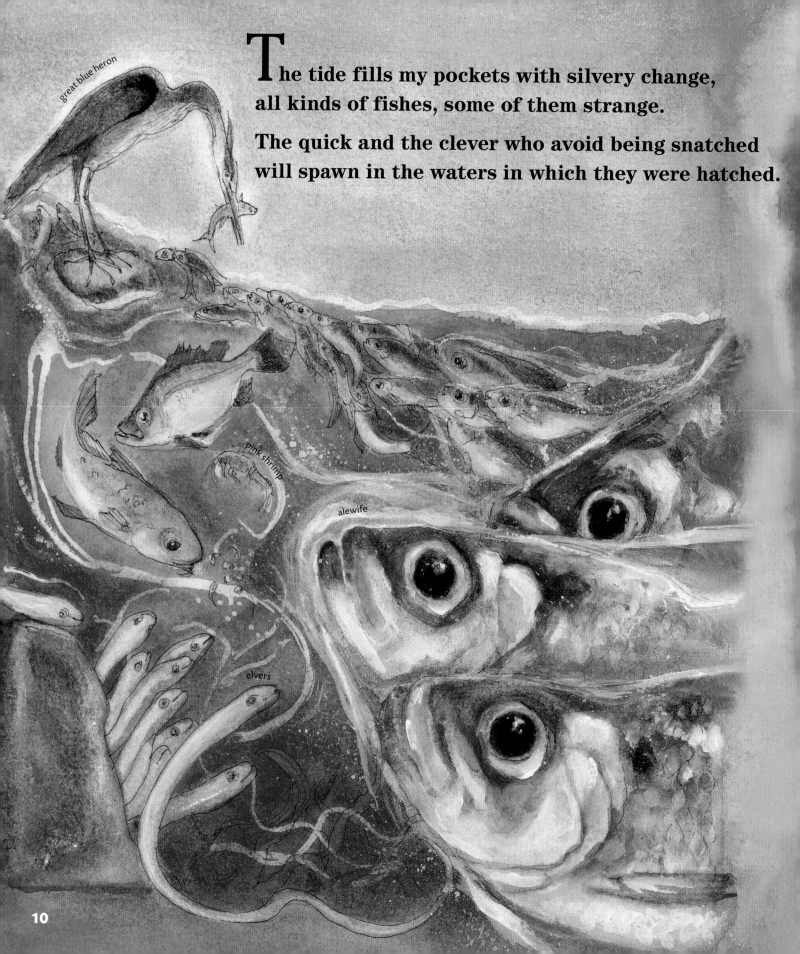

The tide fills my pockets with silvery change,
all kinds of fishes, some of them strange.

The quick and the clever who avoid being snatched
will spawn in the waters in which they were hatched.

great blue heron

pink shrimp

alewife

elvers

10

striped bass

white perch

American shad

shortnose sturgeon

sea lamprey

## Nurseries of the Sea

Most of the fish and shellfish we eat need estuaries to complete their life cycles. Some spend their entire lives in estuaries, while others come and go. The full-timers are small, minnow-sized fish such as mummichogs and sticklebacks. Larger fish visit estuaries to feed or migrate through them to spawn—often in the same rivers or lakes where they were hatched.

Estuaries provide a safe place for young fish to grow. One of the most amazing is the elver, or baby American eel. Elvers swim up East Coast estuaries and rivers after drifting more than 1,000 miles on ocean currents from the Sargasso Sea, where they were hatched. Adult American eels spend up to 20 years in rivers and lakes, then swim all the way back to the Sargasso Sea, where they spawn and die.

$H$orseshoe crabs visit me late on spring nights
to lay eggs in my sand when the tide's at its height.

As soon as the sky in the morning grows light,
hungry birds will find breakfast to power their flight.

Atlantic horseshoe crab

## Horseshoe Crabs: Older than Dinosaurs!

Scientists have found horseshoe crab fossils that are 445 million years old—about 200 million years older than dinosaurs. Horseshoe crabs aren't really crabs at all, but relatives of scorpions and spiders. Unlike their venomous cousins, they don't sting or bite.

During the highest tides in spring, around the full and new moons, horseshoe crabs lay their tiny greenish eggs at night in the sand near the high tide line. One female horseshoe crab can lay nearly 90,000 eggs. Baby horseshoe crabs look like tiny versions of their parents without tails. Horseshoe crabs molt as they grow, and you can sometimes find their empty shells on the beach.

Delaware Bay has the largest breeding population of horseshoe crabs in the world. Shorebirds such as robin-sized red knots depend on horseshoe crab eggs, which are high in fat, to fuel their spring migration from South America to their breeding grounds in the Canadian Arctic. Without horseshoe crab eggs, many shorebirds would disappear.

red knot

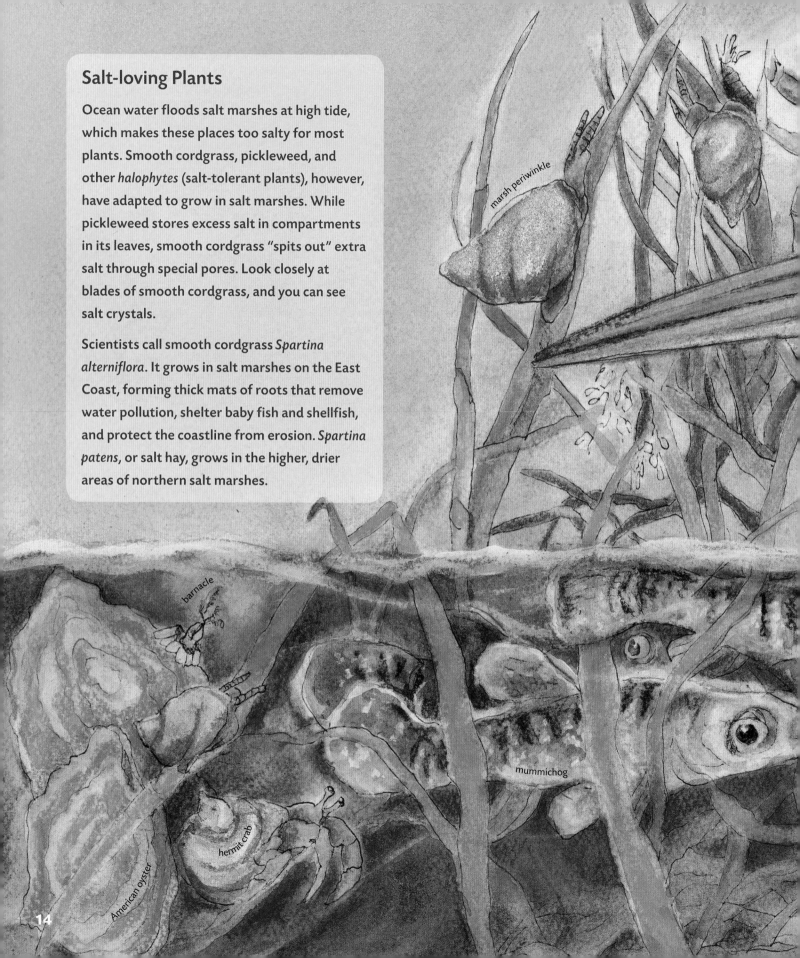

## Salt-loving Plants

Ocean water floods salt marshes at high tide, which makes these places too salty for most plants. Smooth cordgrass, pickleweed, and other *halophytes* (salt-tolerant plants), however, have adapted to grow in salt marshes. While pickleweed stores excess salt in compartments in its leaves, smooth cordgrass "spits out" extra salt through special pores. Look closely at blades of smooth cordgrass, and you can see salt crystals.

Scientists call smooth cordgrass *Spartina alterniflora*. It grows in salt marshes on the East Coast, forming thick mats of roots that remove water pollution, shelter baby fish and shellfish, and protect the coastline from erosion. *Spartina patens*, or salt hay, grows in the higher, drier areas of northern salt marshes.

marsh periwinkle

barnacle

mummichog

hermit crab

American oyster

damselfly

pickleweed

Cordgrass is swishing all over my shores.
Pickleweed covers my soft, sandy floors.

Salt water won't bother these two nifty plants—
they have tricks for growing where other ones can't.

smooth cordgrass

North American river otter

Tough little mummichogs frolic and thrive
in places where other fish wouldn't survive.

They will put up with salt and heat and pollution,
and if my pools dry up, they have a solution.

16

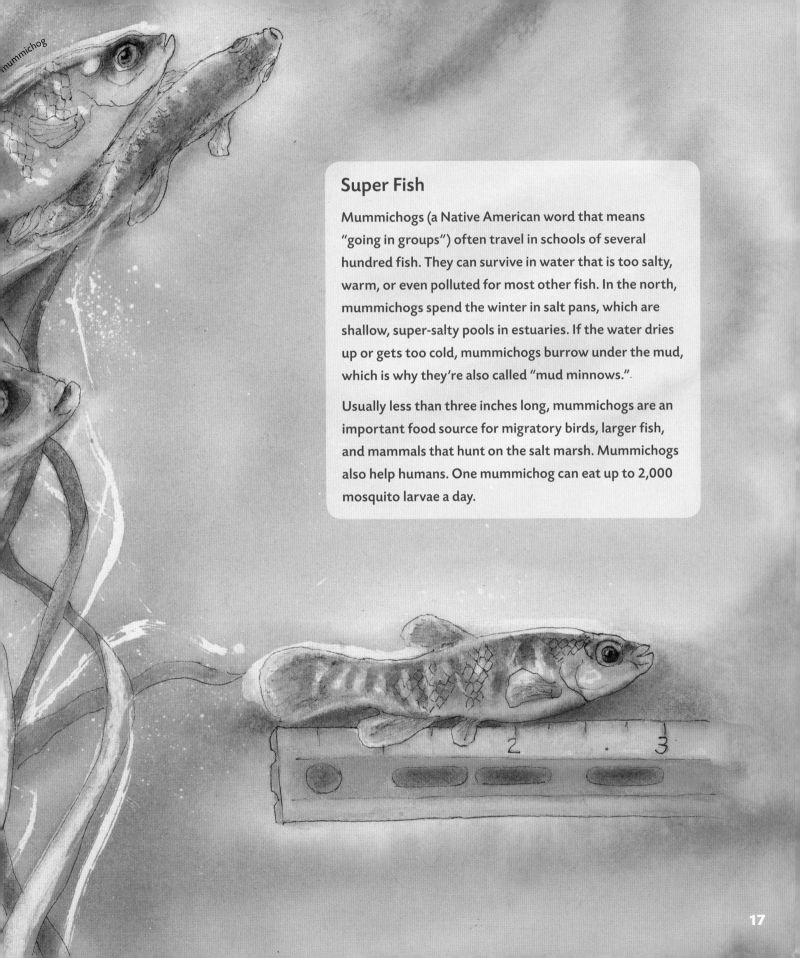

mummichog

## Super Fish

Mummichogs (a Native American word that means "going in groups") often travel in schools of several hundred fish. They can survive in water that is too salty, warm, or even polluted for most other fish. In the north, mummichogs spend the winter in salt pans, which are shallow, super-salty pools in estuaries. If the water dries up or gets too cold, mummichogs burrow under the mud, which is why they're also called "mud minnows."

Usually less than three inches long, mummichogs are an important food source for migratory birds, larger fish, and mammals that hunt on the salt marsh. Mummichogs also help humans. One mummichog can eat up to 2,000 mosquito larvae a day.

## Bloodsuckers

Marsh mosquitoes and greenhead flies breed in salt marshes along estuaries, which can make these places uncomfortable in summer. Only the females bite, because they need protein from blood in order to lay their eggs. These pesky insects may seem of no use, but they are food for birds such as tree swallows, purple martins, and kingbirds. If a greenhead bites you, at least you're doing your part for the food web!

Eastern kingbird

seaside meadow katydid

purple martin

greenhead fly

Midges, mosquitoes, and big greenhead flies
buzz up from my mud and into the sky.

Just a smidge of warm blood is what they must find,
to lay billions of eggs and make more of their kind.

tree swallow

Eastern salt-marsh mosquito

19

If you're quiet and lucky you might hear the crunch
of a terrapin munching a snail for her lunch.

Too many snails can ruin my grass.
Keep chomping, dear turtle, so my marshes will last!

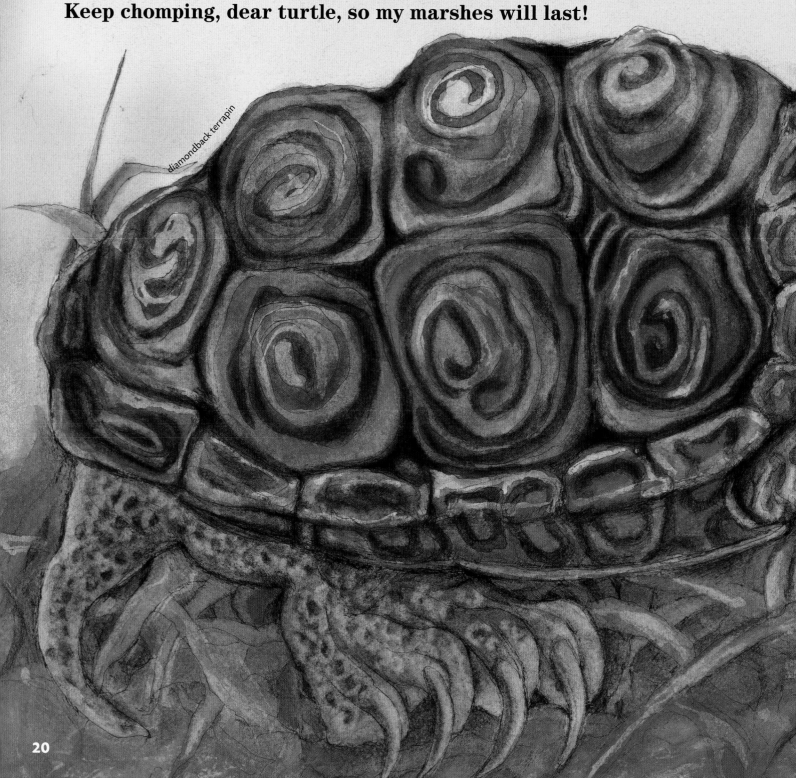

diamondback terrapin

periwinkle

## The Turtle of the Salt Marsh

The diamondback terrapin is the only turtle in the world known to live in brackish water. It is found in salt marshes from Cape Cod to the Gulf Coast. Named for the diamond-shaped rings on its shell and from an Algonquian word for "little turtle," it often has silvery white skin marked with black dots and squiggles. Females, with shells about the size of a salad plate, are much larger than males.

Diamondbacks (along with crabs, fish, and shorebirds) eat marsh periwinkle snails, which scientists have shown can kill large areas of salt marsh when their populations grow too large.

Once hunted almost to extinction for turtle soup, diamondback terrapins face new threats. Thousands drown in crab pots. Many female terrapins are killed by cars while crossing busy roads to lay their eggs on the beach. Today, people are working to help these turtles in programs that hatch terrapin eggs in captivity and release the young turtles when they are too big to be eaten by most predators.

## Life on the Tide Flats

An estuary at low tide might seem empty, but the tide flats are home to many fascinating creatures. They all help keep estuaries healthy.

Ribbed mussels live among smooth cordgrass roots and filter plankton, bacteria, and pollution from huge amounts of estuary water in salt marshes from Massachusetts to Florida. What they filter from the water but don't eat becomes *pseudofeces*—in other words, "fake poop"—which helps fertilize the cordgrass.

On the tide flats, clams, oysters, and blue mussels feed the same way when the tide floods in, and they too produce pseudofeces.

Many kinds of worms live in the mud and sand. Clam worms, which are green and purple and have four eyes, can extend their jaws outside their bodies to catch prey, and if a shorebird catches them, they can break apart and grow new bodies from the broken pieces!

smooth cordgrass

Atlantic ribbed mussel

soft-shell clam

razor clam

hard-shell clam

bloodworm

herring gull

blue mussel

green crab

clam worm

Mussels and oysters and one-footed clams
keep to their beds on my mud, rocks, and sand.

In the muck all around them lurk bristly worms
and other strange creatures that wriggle and squirm.

swamp sparrow

belted kingfisher

osprey

semipalmated plovers

American oystercatcher

double-crested cormorant

dunlin

black-bellied plover

whimbrel

American oyster

## A Banquet for Birds

Millions of migratory shorebirds, such as whimbrels and the small species of sandpipers collectively called peeps, depend on estuaries as critical places to eat and rest during spring and fall migrations. Without estuaries full of invertebrates, fish, and other food, many shorebird species would disappear.

How do all these birds find enough to eat in the estuary? They feed in different areas. Birds with short legs and bills, such as dunlins and plovers, feed at the water's edge on tiny crustaceans and other small invertebrates, while birds with long legs and bills, such as great blue herons, wade into the water to catch fish and other prey. Some shorebirds, such as whimbrels, jab the marsh mud with long beaks that have nerve endings at the tip to feel for prey such as worms.

Whimbrels and plovers and big flocks of peeps
are probing my tide flats for soft-bodied treats.

In fall they must eat as much as they can
to survive long migrations to faraway lands.

dunlin

American avocet

ruddy turnstone

sand shrimp

piping plover

whimbrel

## The Salt Marsh Recycling Crew

Few animals eat living spartina (cordgrass), which dies back in the fall. Fungi and bacteria break down most of this dead grass into *detritus*. Crabs (such as delicious blue crabs) and tiny amphipods (such as shrimp-like beach hoppers) eat this rotten plant material, along with dead animal matter. These and other creatures that eat detritus are called *detritivores*.

One of the most common detritivores in estuaries from Massachusetts to Texas is the fiddler crab. The male has one claw that is much larger than the other, which he waves to attract a female. He looks like he's playing a fiddle when he does this. Fiddlers pick bits of detritus from the mud and stuff it into their mouths. Females can eat twice as fast as males because they can eat with both claws, while males can only use one.

Special bacteria also help clean up estuaries by breaking down dead plants and animals into nutrients. That rotten egg smell in marsh mud is the scent of these bacteria doing their job!

fiddler crab

blue crab

salt-marsh amphipod

My marshes and shores are the most perfect spots
for crabs and other small lovers of rot.

They nibble dead cordgrass and sip stinky goo—
who could ask for a better recycling crew?

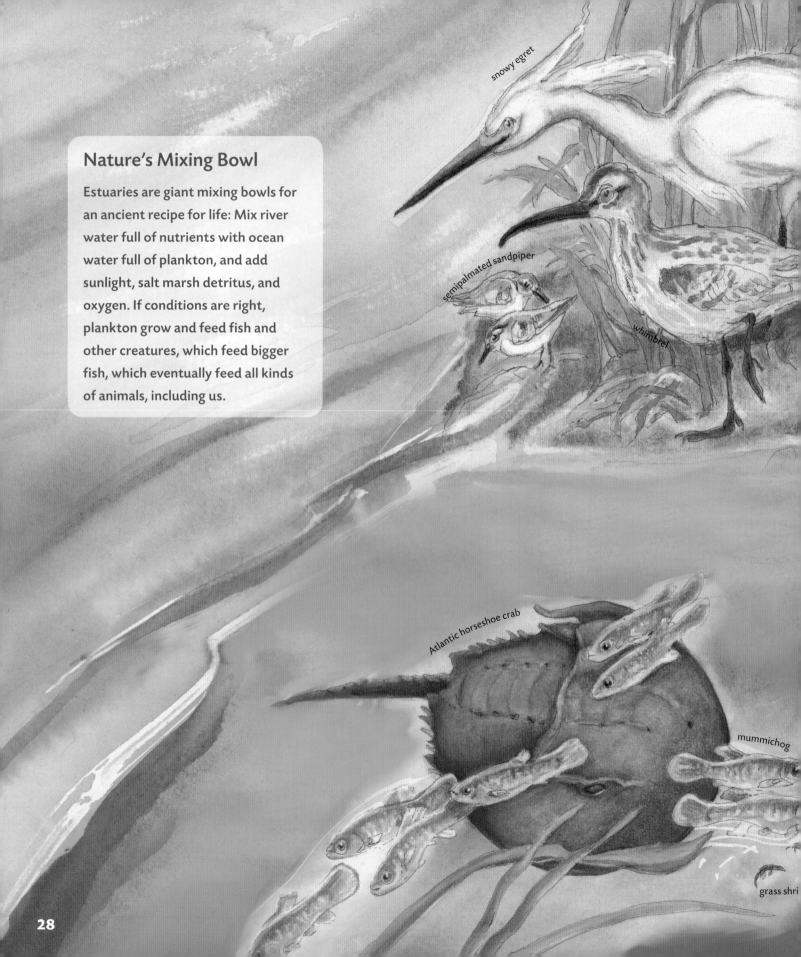

## Nature's Mixing Bowl

Estuaries are giant mixing bowls for an ancient recipe for life: Mix river water full of nutrients with ocean water full of plankton, and add sunlight, salt marsh detritus, and oxygen. If conditions are right, plankton grow and feed fish and other creatures, which feed bigger fish, which eventually feed all kinds of animals, including us.

snowy egret

semipalmated sandpiper

whimbrel

Atlantic horseshoe crab

mummichog

grass shri

Everything mixes and mingles in me,
washed down from the river or up from the sea.

I make it all into something new.
In every season, that's what I do.

## GREAT ESCAPES
## How do estuary creatures avoid predators?

### Hide

Fiddler crabs hide in their burrows and seal themselves inside with a plug of mud to avoid being eaten by fish and blue crabs

when the tide rises. How do fiddlers know when the tide is low and it's safe to come out again? Their body rhythm is tied to the cycle of the moon and the tides. If you take a fiddler crab far away from the ocean, it will still become active at the time of low tide in its original home.

### Stick with the crowd

Like other small fish, mummichogs find safety in numbers, traveling in schools of hundreds of fish. Large schools of identical fish can confuse predators and appear as a much larger fish.

### Blend in

Another way to hide is to blend in with your surroundings. This adaptation is called camouflage. Flounders (flatfish that live on estuary and sea bottoms) can change color to blend in with the mud, sand, and rocks around them. Many shorebirds have earth-toned plumage that helps them hide in

broad daylight right on the beach. The plumage and eggs of the piping plover, an endangered shorebird that nests on the beach and feeds in tide flats, are the color of sand, making them almost impossible for predators to see.

### Break a leg ... and grow a new one

If a predator grabs a crab by a claw or a leg, the crab can release it to escape! Crabs are among a handful of animals that have this amazing ability, which is called *autotomy,* meaning "self-amputation." Crabs will eventually develop a new limb as they grow larger by molting (shedding their shells). The ability to grow a new limb is called *regeneration.*

## Close your shell and hang on tight

Ribbed mussels and blue mussels can't swim or crawl away from predators such as blue crabs and willets. Instead, they keep their shells tightly closed and anchor themselves to rocks, the root structures of spartina, and the shells of other mussels with hundreds of thin, strong byssal threads. A mussel produces these threads by secreting a substance from a gland in its foot. The substance solidifies in seawater, forming strong elastic threads, each of which has a disk at the end where it attaches to a surface.

## Ooze mucus

When threatened, clam worms ooze mucus, which hardens into a protective shell around their bodies. Yuck, right? That's probably how would-be predators react, too!

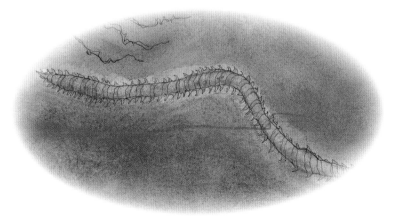

## Keep out of reach

Marsh periwinkles often feed at the base of smooth cordgrass at low tide, but long before the tide comes back in, they begin climbing cordgrass stems to avoid predators such as crabs and fish. How do they know when the tide is returning? They have a built-in clock that tells them.

## Warn your friends

Mud snails feed in large groups on algae that grows on top of marsh mud, following each other's slime trails. When a snail is injured, however, it sends out a chemical that warns other snails in the area to leave.

## Wear your armor

The mollusks that live in estuaries, including mussels, clams, oysters, and snails, use their shells as their first defense against predators. Crabs, like insects, have their skeletons on the outsides of their bodies, and this exoskeleton serves as armor to protect the soft body inside.

## GLOSSARY

**algae** (singular, *alga*) A large and diverse group of photosynthesizing organisms that grow in fresh and salt water and, unlike land plants, have no leaves, stems, or roots. They range in size from phytoplankton to giant kelp, and they include the common seaweeds.

**amphipod** A small crustacean that resembles a shrimp. It is flattened from side to side and has feet that can be used for crawling, hopping, or swimming.

**bacteria** (singular, *bacterium*) Microscopic, single-celled organisms that are able to eat and rapidly multiply. More bacteria live on Earth than any other living thing. Some cause disease, but most help digest food and break down waste into chemicals and nutrients.

**brackish** Water that is somewhat salty, but not as salty as ocean water.

**camouflage** Coloration and patterns that help an animal blend into its surroundings.

**carnivore** A meat-eater.

**consumers** In a food web, organisms that get energy by eating other organisms and can't make food from sunlight.

**crustacean** An animal with a tough outer covering (called an exoskeleton), antennae, and jointed legs. Crabs, lobsters, shrimp, and amphipods are crustaceans.

**decomposers** In a food web, microscopic organisms such as bacteria and fungi that break down dead plant and animal matter and release nutrients back into the soil and water.

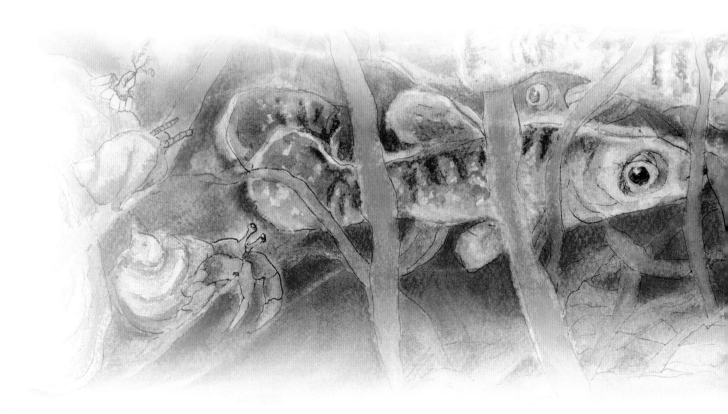

**detritus** In an estuary, particles of dead plant and animal matter that are decomposing.

**detritivore** An animal that eats detritus.

**estuary** A partially enclosed body of water where one or more rivers mix with seawater to create water that is brackish.

**fungi** (singular, *fungus*) Organisms that feed on decaying matter. Fungi include mold, mildew, mushrooms, and yeasts.

**halophyte** A plant that can grow in a salty environment.

**herbivore** A plant eater.

**invertebrate** An animal without a backbone.

**mollusc** An invertebrate with a soft body that is usually protected by a single shell (as in periwinkles, whelks, and other *gastropods*) or two shells (as in clams, mussels, oysters, and other *bivalves*).

**plankton** (singular, *plankter*) Microscopic plants and tiny animals that drift in the ocean and fresh water.

**producers** In a food web, organisms such as algae and plants that can make their own food from sunlight through photosynthesis.

**spartina** A group of salt-tolerant (halophytic) marsh grasses such as smooth cordgrass (*Spartina alterniflora*) and salt-marsh hay (*Spartina patens*).

**wetland** An area where plants grow and the ground is soggy or under shallow water at least part of the time. Marshes, swamps and bogs are wetlands.

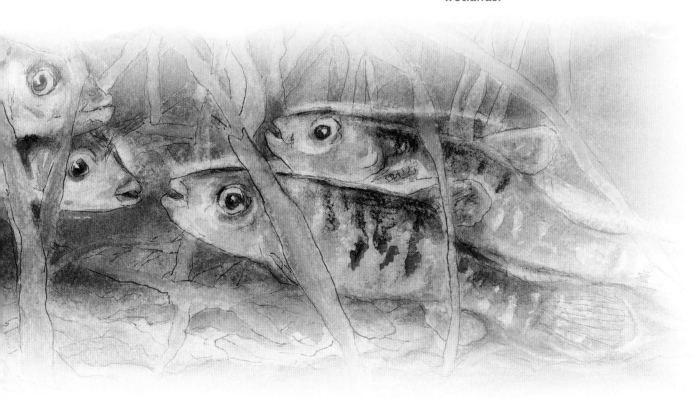

## Meet *The Secret Bay*'s Cast of Characters

All kinds of amazing plants and animals spend part or all of their lives in estuaries, including horseshoe crabs, sea lampreys, and sturgeon, all three of which are among the most ancient creatures on earth. The organisms featured in *The Secret Bay* are just a sampling of the animals and plants you might find in a salt marsh estuary in the U.S. from Maine to the Gulf Coast of Texas, depending on the time of year. Some of the birds and mammals listed here also live in and use other habitats besides estuaries.

### BIRDS *(mostly during spring and fall migrations)*

**American avocet,** *Recurvirostra americana* (page 25)

LENGTH: 16 to 18.5 inches

HABITAT: Salt marsh and freshwater marshes

SEASON: Winter

**American oystercatcher,** *Haematopus palliates* (pages 2, 24)

LENGTH: 15 to 17 inches

HABITAT: Shoreline, southeast U.S. to Gulf Coast

SEASON: Year-round, winters in Florida

**belted kingfisher,** *Megaceryle alcyon* (pages 24, 29 )

LENGTH: 13 inches

HABITAT: Estuaries, lakes, and ponds, with hunting perches over calm, clear water

SEASON: Spring through fall north, year-round south

**black-bellied plover,** *Pluvialis squatarola* (page 24)

LENGTH: 11 inches

HABITAT: Shoreline

SEASON: Late summer and fall north, winter from Virginia to Gulf Coast south

**black-crowned night heron,** *Nycticorax nycticorax* (pages 3, 29)

LENGTH: 25 inches

HABITAT: Brackish wetlands, salt marshes and freshwater marshes

SEASON: Spring through summer, except year-round in Florida

**common tern,** *Sterna hirundo* (page 29)

LENGTH: 12 to 15 inches

HABITAT: Estuaries, shoreline, beaches on Eastern Seaboard to Gulf Coast, Louisiana

SEASON: Spring, summer, and fall, depending on region

**double-crested cormorant,** *Phalacrocorax auritus* (page 24)

LENGTH: 33 inches

HABITAT: Any open water, from oceans to ponds

SEASON: Spring and summer north, year round from Virginia to Florida, winter on Gulf Coast

**dunlin,** *Calidris alpina* (page 24)

LENGTH: 8.5 inches

HABITAT: Shoreline

SEASON: Fall in Maine, winter south to Gulf Coast

**Eastern kingbird,** *Tyrannus tyrannus* (page 18)

LENGTH: 8.5 inches

HABITAT: Grasslands, but hunts for insects in salt marshes

SEASON: Spring and summer

**great blue heron,** *Ardea herodias* (page 10)

LENGTH: 46 inches

HABITAT: Salt marsh and freshwater marshes

SEASON: Spring through fall in the north, year-round south

**great egret,** *Ardea alba* (pages 2, 4, 6, 13, 15)

LENGTH: 39 inches

HABITAT: Salt marshes and freshwater marshes from Southern Canada to Texas Gulf Coast

SEASON: Spring and summer north, year-round south

**herring gull,** *Larus argentatus* (page 23)

LENGTH: 25 inches

HABITAT: Shoreline

SEASON: Year-round

**osprey,** *Pandion haliaetus* (page 24, flying)

LENGTH: 23 inches

HABITAT: Bays, rivers, lakes and ponds

SEASON: Spring and summer north, year-round in Florida, winter on the Gulf Coast Louisiana to Texas

**piping plover,** *Charadrius melodus* (page 25)

LENGTH: 7.25 inches

HABITAT: Shoreline

SEASON: Summer Maine to Virginia, winter south to Gulf Coast

**purple martin,** *Progne subis* (page 18)

LENGTH: 8 inches

HABITAT: Lakes and ponds, but will hunt for insects in salt marsh estuaries

SEASON: Spring and summer

**red knot,** *Calidris canutus* (pages 3, 13)

LENGTH: 10.5 inches

HABITAT: Shoreline

SEASON: Spring, especially in Delaware Bay, winter from Massachusetts south to the Gulf Coast

**ruddy turnstone,** *Arenaria interpres* (page 25)

LENGTH: 9.5 inches

HABITAT: Shoreline

SEASON: Late summer and fall migration north, winter from Massachusetts south to the Gulf Coast

**semipalmated sandpiper,** *Calidris pusilla* (page 28)

LENGTH: 6.25 inches

HABITAT: Shoreline

SEASON: Spring and fall migration

**snowy egret,** *Egretta thula* (page 28)

LENGTH: 24 inches

HABITAT: Salt marsh and freshwater marshes

SEASON: Spring and summer from southern Maine to Georgia, year-round in Florida and Gulf Coast

**swamp sparrow,** *Melospiza georgiana* (page 24)

LENGTH: 5.75 inches

HABITAT: Marshes

SEASON: Summer north, year-round Middle Atlantic coast, winter from Virginia to Gulf Coast

**tree swallow,** *Tachycineta bicolor* (page 19)

LENGTH: 5.75 inches

HABITAT: Marshes and areas near water that produce abundant flying insects such as mosquitoes

SEASON: Spring and summer north, winter south to Gulf Coast

**whimbrel,** *Numenius phaeopus* (pages 25, 28)

LENGTH: 17.5 inches

HABITAT: Shoreline and mudflats in winter

SEASON: Spring and fall north, winter south to Gulf Coast

## FISH

**alewife (herring),** *Alosa pseudoharengus* (page 10)

LENGTH: 10 to 12 inches

HABITAT: Estuaries, oceans, and rivers at different times of the year, from Newfoundland to the Carolinas

SEASON: Easiest to see in spring, when adults migrate from the ocean up rivers to spawn. Juveniles migrate from fresh to salt water summer through fall.

**American eel/elvers,** *Anguilla rostrata* (page 10, elvers)

LENGTH: Females up to 5 feet. Males up to 2 feet

HABITAT: Estuaries, freshwater rivers and ponds, and ocean, depending on stage of life cycle

SEASON: In spring, tiny elvers (baby eels, also called glass eels) swim from the ocean into estuaries. In fall, mature eels, after living between 3 and 40 years in fresh or brackish water, swim through estuaries on their way to spawn in the Sargasso Sea.

**American shad,** *Alosa sapidissima* (page 11)

LENGTH: 12 to 25 inches

HABITAT: Estuaries, fresh water, and ocean depending on stage of life cycle, from Newfoundland to the Gulf of Mexico

SEASON: Spring, when shad migrate from the ocean up rivers to spawn

**mummichog, *Fundulus heteroclitus***
(pages 4, 6, 8, 14-15, 16, 28)

LENGTH: Up to 6 inches (but most are 3 inches or smaller, and females are larger than males)

HABITAT: Shallow, brackish water such as salt marsh creeks, salt pans and eelgrass beds, Newfoundland to Florida

SEASON: Year-round

**sea lamprey, *Petromyzon marinus***
(page 11)

LENGTH: Up to 3 feet

HABITAT: Rivers (juveniles), ocean (adults), St. Lawrence River to northern Florida

SEASON: Adults migrate through estuaries in spring from the ocean up rivers. Juveniles migrate through estuaries late fall through early spring to the ocean.

**shortnose sturgeon, *Acipenser brevirostrum*** (page 11)

LENGTH: Up to 4 feet. Its larger cousin, the Atlantic sturgeon, can grow up to 14 feet long.

HABITAT: Rivers and estuaries, New Brunswick to Florida

SEASON: Summer

**striped bass, *Morone saxatilis***
(page 11)

LENGTH: Up to 59 inches

HABITAT: Estuaries and the ocean

HABITAT: Spring and summer (adults), year-round (juveniles), Canada to Florida

**white perch, *Morone americana***
(page 11)

LENGTH: 6 to 10 inches

HABITAT: Estuaries and fresh water, depending on lifecycle and season, New Jersey to South Carolina.

HABITAT: Much of the year in estuaries, but these fish migrate upstream to spawn in freshwater rivers in spring and early summer.

## ARTHROPODS

**Atlantic horseshoe crab, *Limulus polyphemus*** (pages 4, 12, 28)

LENGTH: 14 to 19 inches (females are larger)

HABITAT: Estuaries and ocean from Maine to the Yucatan Peninsula in Mexico

SEASON: Spring

## CRUSTACEANS

**blue crab, *Callinectes sapidus***
(pages 5, 27)

LENGTH: Up to 9 inches wide

HABITAT: Bays and brackish estuaries, Nova Scotia to Argentina

SEASON: Year-round

**European green crab, *Carcinus maenus*** (page 23, in gull's beak)

LENGTH: 3 inches wide

HABITAT: Shallow water and tide flats, moves to deeper water in winter, Nova Scotia to New Jersey. This crab is an invasive species transported to America from Europe, and it eats young clams, damaging the soft-shell clam fishery.

SEASON: Year-round

**fiddler crab, *Uca* species**
(pages 21, 26)

LENGTH: About 1.5 inches wide

HABITAT: Low, wet areas of salt marsh from Cape Cod to Texas

SEASON: Year-round

**grass shrimp, *Palaemonetes* species** (page 29)

LENGTH: 1 to 2 inches long

HABITAT: Salt marshes, submerged seaweed on sandy-muddy bottoms, ditches

SEASON: Year-round

**hermit crab, *Pagurus* species**
(page 4)

LENGTH: up to 1.5 inches

HABITAT: Shallow waters, mudflats, and beaches

SEASON: Year-round

**pink shrimp,** *Penaeus duorarum* (page 10)

**LENGTH:** 6 to 8 inches (females are larger)

**HABITAT:** Juveniles live in estuaries for 2 to 6 months from the lower Chesapeake Bay to the Gulf of Mexico. They gradually migrate to open ocean, where they grow into adults and spawn. Larvae drift into estuaries and the cycle begins again.

**SEASON:** Varies, depending on life stage.

**salt marsh amphipod,** *Orchestia grillus* (page 27)

**LENGTH:** Less than 1 inch

**HABITAT:** Lives around salt marsh grasses

**SEASON:** Most of the year

**sand shrimp,** *Crangon septemspinosa* (page 25)

**LENGTH:** Up to 2.75 inches

**HABITAT:** Salt marshes, eelgrass beds, submerged seaweeds on sandy bottoms

**SEASON:** Year-round, but moves to deeper water in winter

## INSECTS

**damselfly, such as marsh bluet (male),** *Enallagma erbium* (page 15)

**LENGTH:** Less than 1.25 inches

**HABITAT:** Marshes, lakes, and ponds in New England

**SEASON:** Summer

**Eastern salt-marsh mosquito,** *Aedes sollicitans* (pages 18–19)

**LENGTH:** Less than 0.25 inch

**HABITAT:** Salt marshes along the Eastern Seaboard from Canada to the Gulf Coast, up to 5 miles inland

**SEASON:** Spring through fall, depending on region

**greenhead fly,** *Tabanus nigrovittatus* (page 18)

**LENGTH:** 0.85 to 1.15 inches

**HABITAT:** Salt marshes on Eastern Seaboard

**SEASON:** Summer

**seaside meadow katydid or salt-marsh grasshopper,** *Orchelimum fidicinium* (page 18)

**LENGTH:** Just under 0.75 inch

**HABITAT:** Salt marsh

**SEASON:** Summer

## WORMS

**bloodworm,** *Glycera dibranchiata* (page 22)

**LENGTH:** Up to 15 inches

**HABITAT:** Burrowed in mudflats from the Gulf of St. Lawrence to the Gulf of Mexico

**SEASON:** Year-round

**clam worm, sandworm, polychaete worm,** *Nereis* species (page 22)

**LENGTH:** Up to 7.5 inches

**HABITAT:** Burrowed in mudflats, Atlantic and Pacific coasts

**SEASON:** Year-round

## MOLLUSCS

### Gastropods (one shell)

**marsh periwinkle,** *Littorina irrorata* (pages 2, 6, 7, 14, 20, 22)

**LENGTH:** Up to 1 inch

**HABITAT:** Wet areas of salt marsh, usually on cordgrass stems, New York to Gulf Coast of Texas

**SEASON:** Year-round

### Bivalves (two shells)

**American oyster,** *Crassostrea virginica* (pages 5, 24)

**LENGTH:** Up to 10 inches

**HABITAT:** In "beds" below the low tide line on hard, non-shifting surfaces of estuaries from the Gulf of St. Lawrence to the Gulf of Mexico

**SEASON:** Year-round

**Atlantic ribbed mussel,** *Geukensia demissa* (page 22)

**LENGTH:** Up to 4 inches

**HABITAT:** Lodged among spartina stems and roots in estuaries and salt marshes from the Gulf of Maine to Florida

**SEASON:** Year-round

**blue mussel,** *Mytilus edulis* (page 23)

**LENGTH:** 2 to 4 inches

**HABITAT:** In beds in the intertidal zone (between high and low tides) and in shallow waters from northern Canada to South Carolina

**SEASON:** Year-round

**hard-shell clam or quahog,**
*Mercenaria mercenaria* (page 22)

**LENGTH:** 1 to 4 inches

**HABITAT:** Burrowed just below the sand between the tide lines and in shallow water from Canada to Florida

**SEASON:** Year-round

**razor clam,** *Ensis directus* (page 22)

**LENGTH:** Up to 10 inches (about six times longer than wide)

**HABITAT:** Sandy and muddy bottoms of bays and estuaries from Labrador to South Carolina

**SEASON:** Year-round

**soft-shell clam,** *Mya arenaria* (page 22)

**SIZE:** Up to 4 inches long

**HABITAT:** Buried in mud or sand in estuaries and bays from Labrador to North Carolina

**SEASON:** Year-round

## REPTILES

**diamondback terrapin,**
*Malaclemys* **species** (pages 20–21)

**LENGTH:** Females up to 11 inches, males up to 5.5 inches

**HABITAT:** Salt marshes and tidal creeks from Cape Cod to Corpus Christi, Texas

**SEASON:** Year-round

## MAMMALS

**North American river otter,**
*Lontra canadensis* (pages 5, 16, 29)

Length: 3 to 4 feet

**HABITAT:** Wetlands, including salt-marsh estuaries, from Canada to Texas coast

**SEASON:** Year-round

**Raccoon,** *Procyon lotor* (page 5)

**LENGTH:** 2 to 3 feet

**HABITAT:** Salt marshes, tide flats, shores, searching for food

**SEASON:** Year-round

## PLANKTON

**Phytoplankton** (page 9)

**SIZE:** Microscopic, from less than 1 to more than 100 microns in diameter. (A micron is one-millionth of a meter; one thousand microns equals a millimeter, which is the smallest size that can be seen with the naked eye.)

**HABITAT:** The top, sunlit layer of water in estuaries, oceans, and fresh water bodies in temperate regions

**SEASON:** Most abundant in spring, least abundant in winter (due to low sunlight) depending on region

**Zooplankton** (page 9)

**SIZE:** From less than 2 microns to more than 200 millimeters (8 inches)

**HABITAT:** Most of these floating animals are tiny and include copepods and larval forms of crustaceans, fish, jellyfish, urchins, sea stars, and some marine snails and worms. They live near the surface of the water, where they feed on phytoplankton and each other.

**SEASON:** Mostly spring and summer, but present in other seasons depending on region

## PLANTS

**pickleweed or glasswort,**
*Salicornia* **species** (page 15)

**LENGTH:** Less than 1 foot

**HABITAT:** Salt marshes

**SEASON:** Spring and summer, turns red in fall

**salt-meadow hay,** *Spartina patens* (pages 4–5, 6–7)

**LENGTH:** Up to 2 feet

**HABITAT:** High salt marsh, Newfoundland to Texas

**SEASON:** Spring and summer (dies back in fall)

**smooth cordgrass,** *Spartina alterniflora* (pages 4–5, 6–7, 13, 14, 18–19, 20, 22, 24, 28–29 )

Length: Up to 8 feet

**HABITAT:** Wet areas of salt marshes along the Eastern Seaboard from Newfoundland to Northern Florida and in the Gulf of Mexico from parts of Florida to Texas

**SEASON:** Spring and summer (dies back in fall)

Dear Reader,

I've always loved exploring "secret" places that many people don't even notice. When I was nine years old, I wandered out onto the salt marsh to hunt for shells behind the cottage my family rented in Wells Beach, Maine. I didn't know what an estuary was back then, but out on the marsh I fell in love with these magical places.

Many years later, I wrote about scientists studying estuaries and learned how important these places are to life on Earth. The more I learned about estuaries, the more I grew to love them—and to worry about their future. That's what inspired me to write this book.

Researching *The Secret Bay* has opened my eyes not only to the wonders of estuaries, but also to how human activity has harmed them. People have dumped garbage and sewage into estuaries, filled salt marshes with dirt to build houses, and drained these important wetlands to try to control mosquitoes. Anything that leaks into rivers or is washed into them by rain ends up in an estuary. In addition, rising sea levels due to climate change threaten salt marshes along estuaries around the world.

There is hopeful news, however. Understanding how we humans affect estuaries is inspiring people to protect and try to restore them. People are cleaning up estuaries, restoring fish runs and salt marshes, replacing invasive species with native ones, and protecting habitat for fish, birds, and other creatures. With a little help, some estuaries can begin to heal themselves.

To learn more and get involved, visit the National Estuarine Research Reserve System's (NERRS) Estuary Education website at http://estuaries.noaa.gov/Default.aspx. Another fun way to participate is to celebrate National Estuaries Day on the last Saturday in September.

The estuary I explored as a girl is now part of the Wells National Estuarine Research Reserve, which protects 2,250 acres of coastal habitat in southern Maine. Every time I visit the Wells Reserve and other estuaries I feel deeply grateful for these amazing places. This book is my love letter to estuaries and an invitation to you. I hope it inspires you to visit and help care for the wet and wonderful places around your home.

—*Kim Ridley*

## Acknowledgments

### Kim

Thanks to Suzanne Kahn, Education Director of the Wells National Estuarine Research Reserve; Dr. Pamela Morgan, Chair, Department of Environmental Studies at the University of New England; and Dr. David Porter, Professor Emeritus, Department of Plant Biology, University of Georgia, for reviewing the text and so generously sharing their expertise. Deepest gratitude to my writers' group—Ellen Booraem, Jean Fogelberg, Ann Logan, Becky McCall, Gail Page, and Susa Wuorinen—for their brilliance and good humor in critiquing many revisions of this story. Thanks also to my young readers—including my niece, Ivy Curry, and Mae Qi Morgan-Richardson—whose questions and comments were a great help. Thank you to my dear friend and artist Rebekah Raye for bringing the Estuary so magically to life with her art, and to Jonathan Eaton of Tilbury House Publishers for helping to bring this book into the world. Finally, heartfelt thanks to Thomas Curry, a brilliant painter and co-adventurer whose love and belief make all the difference.

### Rebekah

A special thank you to Captain Doug Maple for his friendship and his knowledge of the birds, history, and beautiful estuarine waters of Cedar Key, Florida; and to my husband, Kenny, who makes sharing the many wonders of nature together so joyful through his photography, encouragement, and companionship.

*For my mother, Judy, and always, for Thomas. —KR*

*For Margaret A. Woisard, with gratitude for her love and sharing many inspiring nature walks and trips to Barn Island Estuary. —RR*

TILBURY HOUSE PUBLISHERS
12 Starr Street
Thomaston, Maine 04861
800-582-1899 • www.tilburyhouse.com

Text © 2015 Kimberly Ridley
Illustrations © 2015 Rebekah Raye
Hardcover ISBN 978-088448-433-2
eBook ISBN 978-9-88448-434-9

15 16 17 18 19 20  4CM   10 9 8 7 6 5 4 3 2 1

Library of Congress Cataloging-in-Publication Data
Ridley, Kimberly, author.
 The secret bay / Kimberly Ridley ; Illustrated by Rebekah Raye.
     pages cm
 Audience: Ages 6–11.
 Summary: "A look at estuaries, their importance, and the organisms that live there."—Provided by publisher.
 ISBN 978-0-88448-433-2 (hardcover)
 1.  Estuarine ecology—Juvenile literature. 2.  Estuaries—Juvenile literature.  I. Raye, Rebekah, illustrator. II. Title.
 QH541.5.E8R53 2015
 577.7'86—dc23
                    2015019734

Designed by Faith Hague
Printed in Shenzhen, China by Shenzhen Caimei Printing Co., Ltd.. through Four Colour Print Group, Louisville, Kentucky (July 2015) 54802-0

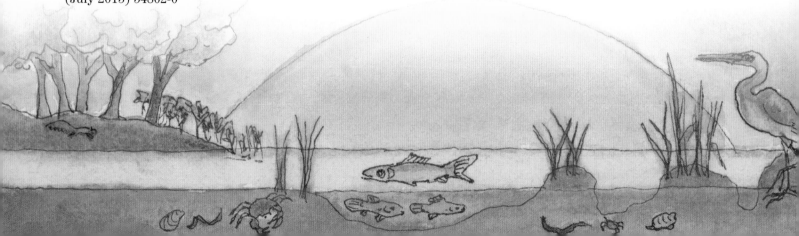